# my last letters

## of a dying summer

TYLER JAMES LANGHORN

The content associated with this book is the sole work and responsibility of the author. Gatekeeper Press had no involvement in the generation of this content.

My Last Letters: Of a Dying Summer

Published by Gatekeeper Press
7853 Gunn Hwy., Suite 209
Tampa, FL 33626
www.GatekeeperPress.com



The cover design, interior formatting, typesetting, and editorial work for this book are entirely the product of the author. Gatekeeper Press did not participate in and is not responsible for any aspect of these elements.

10 9 8 7 6 5 4 3 2 1

ISBN (paperback): 9781662945823

to my dad- for being my favorite poet
my mom- for wanting to write and telling me to do so
my sister- for reading my poems & always being here
my Uncle Oscar- the closest thing I'll have to a grandfather
all of my aunts, uncles, and cousins- I love you
and to Jamie McCarthy- for letting me write poems in english
class & reviewing them on the weekend

Thank you so, so much.

& to April Griffin, William Vogan, Jamie Turner & Griff Fleenor, people
who believe in me and in my work and tell me to keep going

Thank You For Your Contributions:

Encompass Entertainment
Humble Hustle & The Collective
Gabrielle Langhorn
Sharon Langhorn
Jayson Langhorn
Jamie & Chelsea Turner
Griff Fleenor
Jaret White
Abbi Goose
Skya Diaz
Jeffrey Ketron
Robert Linkenhoker
Katherine Whatley
Floyd Johnson
Brianna Mobley
Lynsey Grace
Adam Daniels
Nora Leyes
Dr. Jim and Annie Pontuso
Dr. Pam Fox
UPLS
Hampden-Sydney College
Texas Tavern
RND Coffee
Jack Brown's Roanoke
Starbucks on ATL Highway
Not just God, but Jesus Christ

*Maybe I'll lay down for a little,*
*'Stead of always trying to figure everything out.*
*And all I do is say sorry*
*Half the time, I don't even know what I'm saying it about.*

*Good news, good news, good news*
*That's all they wanna hear*
*No, they don't like it when I'm down*
*But when I'm flying, oh, it make 'em so uncomfortable*
*So different, what's the difference?*

-

*Good News by*
*Malcolm James "Mac Miller" McCormick*

*"if you've never stared off into the distance,*
*then your life is a shame"*

-

*Mrs. Potter's Lullaby*
*Counting Crows*

This body of work commemorates emotions, thoughts, and feelings felt during one of the hottest summers in recorded history. These poems and writings are just that: poems and writings. I found myself in many of these pieces, and I hope that you find something too.

with love,
ty james

# MY LAST LETTERS

A series of poems:

LOVE OR SOMETHING

LIKE IT

other writings:

ABOUT EXISTING

& essays

ABOUT EVERYTHING

ELSE

These are my last letters to my lost lovers. The last letters of this waning, dying summer. After this, I'll find the one who's always there beside me when my restless days are done. When my reckless days are over, I'll lay looking at the sun, thanking the Lord who sent me, that **I finally found the one.**

I want to wrap you up like linen sheets do moving feet on sleepless nights;
A comfort that you don't want to escape just manipulate until it's right.
Cold side of the pillow, hold me,
Swallow me like pills that make you drift to dreams.
And sleep,
Nestled in my arms like a prayer inside the organ that hides behind my ribs.
Swell, deflate, and swell,
The sweet scent of you nearby not lost on me,
These sleepless nights,
Chosen because I never want to leave.
To hold you forever ***I would never sleep***
***Again.***

I wish I could crawl into a ***corner*** and pretend that it was love. That the place where two walls meet the floor was just enough. Like laying awake in that loft with you, softly sawing wood. That floor boards meeting dry wall felt like only your arms could.

**cor**
**ner.**

Why do I live with this feeling that
***everyone else gets to be happy?***
Why do I make my happiness
second fiddle to everyone else's?
What's the secret to ***selfish*** and
who do I need to meet to tell me it?

orange neon
leave your little light on.
tell me you don’t like
to sleep alone

loft downtown
lost my heart downtown
nowhere on this planet
feels like home

***tough luck, junior***

We move on.

Are these feelings lost to me forever? Are they lost to you hiding away like polaroids from a pen pal turned lover, turned wife to another? Are my feelings for you buried somewhere beneath my ribs kept separate from the place where true love will one day live? Is that love, *will that love*, be any different than this? Is this even love? Or do I not even know what love is? ***does love like my poetry even exist?***

i think of you in hand me downs,
afternoons in ***Boone***
i think of you when i'm feeling down
laying in my room
i think of you in tennis balls
bootleggers on the porch
i think of you when i think of love
and not loving you more

We could build a life like sandcastles
Come dodge the waves with me
Decorate our walls with shells
We’ve stolen from the sea
1 billion tiny grains
Of sand and you and me
Hand in hand we’ll ***face the tides***
Building up our dream

Maybe I'm cursed to never know a love that doesn't come with pain attached to it. Maybe I'll blame that on my parents inability to maintain a marriage but their unique ability to remain friends. Maybe my mind is warped to believe that there's a pain present even when there isn't. Maybe this is why I'm more comfortable with upfront love bombing. The distance in "taking it slow" feels indifferent. ***Obsession feels certain.*** My life has been so chaotic that crazy feels nurturing and a normal pace is lagging and lacks excitement. Maybe I need to be loved crazily or not loved at all. That's how it feels. It feels like I'm not loved at all.

I go to bed drunk
And ***I pray for you***
Room still spinning
I lay down and say a prayer for you:
        I pray that life is easy
        I pray it treats you kind
I tell God I hope it's in his plans
That He will make you mine
                                        And I'm *fiiiine*
If that day never comes to pass
But            I pray that you're loved
               And I pray that it lasts
I pray that your husband's
On the full side of the glass
Because a life with you is over flowing
And I'd hate to beat his ass

Somewhere in the fullness of your smile was a note that said it had been a minute.
Not since we'd seen each other,
Of course, a decade had passed,
But since your lips had held that crescent shape and your heart had made that sacred rhythm.
How many days since the blush on your unmarked cheeks was natural, since tension dropped from you shoulders from laughter,
That Jericho walls fell because trumpets of comfort blasted?
That note said it had been a minute since you truly felt seen.
That note was folded like a high school lovers letter and postmarked for that moment in time.
How long has it truly been?
And why did it feel that that smile was just for me?
Could it have been, truly?
Somewhere in the conversation we found comfort and lost track of time.
Something so funny happened that I had to spit out my water but we can only remember my reaction.
What I would give to go back in time and make you my only attraction knowing now,
That reconnection would feel the way it does.
***we should have met for coffee years ago.***

This is a place for you to write things you love about yourself; be as kind to yourself as you possibly can.

I want to hold you close to me
Barefoot in the river
A cold beer can still in your hand
Pressed against my back.
I want to kiss you as the rain starts
And not leave the stream
Until the rain stops.
You're my ***summer dream***
On the banks of blue ridge running water
Nestled in the mountains
Where the cool air settles in the holler.

Will you go with me,
In the search for what we're looking for? Maybe we don't find it. Maybe it's elusive.
Maybe it's the search itself, and if in it we find self;
Maybe you find you're in love with someone else,
I hope that someone else is me.

I hope I've been nestled in the back of your mind like a book turned sideways on a shelf,
discovered by a librarian undertaking the tedious project of realigning the stacks,
finding me in the back to realize I'm the story you've been looking for. I hope you spend
afternoons with me curled up in a window seat, flipping through my pages, sipping tea. Learning, realizing, discovering, that I've been the long lost arc full of adventure that you've always wanted.
I hope you hold me close, bend my pages, write notes in my margins so that you remember through the ages
which parts were your favorite. I hope you never put me down; if and when you do, I hope it's on your night stand, so that I'm right there at nights end and the first thing you grab when the windows let light in.
I hope you carry me in your bag when you're done reading me the first time. To read me again, to reference, to share
in the way we share our favorite book: not to loan them out, but to always have them close by to show our favorite parts.

I hope that you have trouble picking which part is
your favorite because there's always another one
that comes to mind when you say it.
Maybe I'm asking too much. I'd be happy to be a book
you read once, loved, and left on your shelf collecting
dust.
Only to be rediscovered every third summer and
read through and put back. At least I'm nearby and
know you loved me.
Maybe I could live with only that, being someone you
held once.
But I want more than that. I want so much ***more
than that.***

that hotel where we watched the sun
crawl across the room
the Christmas gift I gave
that no one gave to you
i knew that you loved me then
i couldn't find it true
to go back and say i love you
what i wouldn't do

***[framed memories]***

nostalgia hits, like heroin.
could-have-beens are carried winds.
losses hang like carried wins, wondering where the team has been
muscles in your back growing thin from all the weight of life atop your shoulders.

growing older: catastrophe calamity of schedules never matching.
never so in sync, “next week or month or year we’ll meet”

“of course”
lives metro station busy.
radio silence, tv static, satellite direction, dial up connection

"can you call me?"

busy tones the colors of nights alone,
blue light lives reflecting casting shadows on the wall.
***are you still watching?***

Heart shaped shadows are your name across my
paper in a letter that I'm writing and will hand
deliver later to a lover of the light who could only
make life better, she's the sound of the sun rising
she's the flavor of forever
She is perfect
and ***I cannot wait to meet her.***

*(spoiler: this book is not about her
or anyone in particular, really)*

One day they'll read this letter as inspiration, a look at the journey that was my life. I want to say to the person who's fighting to keep going: *keep going*. I also want to say, that if you choose my trajectory as your template, you've got to be content with simply just being chill. I have spent a lot of time taking inventory of the subtle beauties of the world, I've looked at the things around me for which I'm grateful. I take lovers, write poems, spend afternoons analyzing the feelings lent to me from a bottle and a half of champagne- not to mention grass, mushrooms, and small sheets of paper with the nectar of the 20th centuries tiniest discoveries. This is not the path of someone who refuses to cease until they've met success, but someone who knows they're destined for success and finds value in the rest. I'm walking the path to greatness, but stopping to smell the roses, pick them, and deliver them to a house we passed a few miles back because the woman out front had eyes the shade of blue that I've only seen in a dream. My first love told me my life would suck if I never stopped to smell the roses. If only she could see me now, or then, laying in a garden behind a home the size of the cul-de-sac we used to lay in and paint day dreams on the ceiling of my 97 jeep Cherokee Laredo. I made it, see? I made it. I'm at the top of the mountain, laying in a garden.

I say all of this to say: if you choose this path for inspiration, be comfortable in taking the time that leaves you inspired.

---

An allusion 

May I trouble you for a cigarette?

I don't really smoke but it's socially acceptable to ask a stranger for a favor when you two share an addiction

Would you like to get a drink with me?
Or coffee if you don't drink?
Or maybe take a walk with me?
Or maybe take a walk with me,
And realize that I don't think
I'm really worth talking about as much
As others talk to me,

I'm pretending.

I'm pretending.

And these thoughts galavant behind my eye lids through halls as wide as southern rivers
Around tables the size of islands
They parade themselves through city streets of towns with names you can't pronounce and culminate in conclusions you would seem insane to denounce

so you accept them

One day they'll read this letter as inspiration, a look at the journey that was my life. I want to say to the person who's fighting to keep going: *keep going*. I also want to say, that if you choose my trajectory as your template, you've got to be content with simply just being chill. I have spent a lot of time taking inventory of the subtle beauties of the world, I've looked at the things around me for which I'm grateful. I take lovers, write poems, spend afternoons analyzing the feelings lent to me from a bottle and a half of champagne- not to mention grass, mushrooms, and small sheets of paper with the nectar of the 20th centuries tiniest discoveries. This is not the path of someone who refuses to cease until they've met success, but someone who knows they're destined for success and finds value in the rest. I'm walking the path to greatness, but stopping to smell the roses, pick them, and deliver them to a house we passed a few miles back because the woman out front had eyes the shade of blue that I've only seen in a dream. My first love told me my life would suck if I never stopped to smell the roses. If only she could see me now, or then, laying in a garden behind a home the size of the cul-de-sac we used to lay in and paint day dreams on the ceiling of my 97 jeep Cherokee Laredo. I made it, see? I made it. I'm at the top of the mountain, laying in a garden.

I say all of this to say: if you choose this path for
inspiration, be comfortable in taking the time that
leaves you inspired.

---

Some
**Saturdays** are aimless

I slept until almost noon
Or 11. Regardless, the morning was gone

I ran in the park with no rhythm and got chased by a dog in a neighborhood

I built a house out of sticks to make myself feel like a kid again. Some people are calling that "nurturing my inner child"                I'm burying my current pain

I came home and took a shower. Maybe I'd be successful if it was colder

I decided the 4 o'clock hour sucks anyway so I slept from 3:59 to 5:09

I awoke thinking about how my life has felt like one long Saturday on the weekend when my mom has custody but the internet is off, it's raining in the morning, and she goes to the store and leaves me at home, the sun comes out and I can't go outside until she comes back
It's 5:30 and she's not back yet. I lay around the living room waiting to go to my dads on Tuesday, wishing this weekend was one with him because we'd be fishing, or watching a movie

I'm 28 wishing I could go to my dads on Tuesday, wishing this was a weekend with him; we could go fishing, or watch a movie

I wish I could pull myself from this sliver of my queen sized bed covered with laundry

Napping beside my unchecked to do list
I must have a kink for sleeping with disappointment
Or my ex did and I got it from her because here I still am

I used to judge others for spending their last dollars on weed

But the only walk I want to take today is down the wine isle

Champagne bubbles have a way of elevating any afternoon,
effervescent depression with stimulating music is better than the nihilistic acceptance and napping the day away, right?

At least a buzz feels productive

I'll have to explain that sentence to my therapist

It feels too heavy to carry this, so I sit it down
Maybe drowning is my element
So when I'm feeling down
I'm actually high atop an elephant
Looking at the ground
But the ring that I keep seeing isn't the cusp of a crown
But is the big top
And I am just a clown
In a circus for a moment when I'm not feeling down

Is an illusion

An allusion



May I trouble you for a cigarette?

I don't really smoke but it's socially acceptable to ask a stranger for a favor when you two share an addiction

Would you like to get a drink with me?
Or coffee if you don't drink?
Or maybe take a walk with me?
Or maybe take a walk with me,
And realize that I don't think
I'm really worth talking about as much
As others talk to me,

I'm pretending.

I'm pretending.

And these thoughts galavant behind my eye lids through halls as wide as southern rivers
Around tables the size of islands
They parade themselves through city streets of towns with names you can't pronounce and culminate in conclusions you would seem insane to denounce

so you accept them

"I'm lazy... because all I did today, was sleep"

But I'm alone at "home" on Saturday so who's here to care for me but me?

Except no one is coming
Home at 6:30 to put a pizza in the oven and turn on the tv
And there's no home to look forward to on Tuesday
At least
I can have a glass of champagne and watch a dvd
And for a moment
Something else in the room is spinning
Not just me

And that to do list is a distant disappointment that can wait

Productivity feels such a silly high to chase when all I really want to do

Is feel at home again.

Eyes dilated wide, waiting for the best to come.
I've heard great things are worth waiting for so I'm hanging on,
***Hopeful***.

These cigarettes
Sure do taste
Like letting go
Knowing how I used
To hate so much
The smell of smoke
Getting back to being
A version of myself
I've never known
6 cold hearted summers
Do you think that I have grown?

Why do I live with this feeling that ***everyone else gets to be happy?*** Why do I make my happiness second fiddle to everyone else's? What's the secret to ***selfish*** and who do I need to meet to tell me it?

**Amendment :**

There is no happiness. Nothing is worth having. You take the chance to be selfish and get burned regardless. Maybe all that's real is the moment; this moment sucks. Don't try to do anything.

[boy was I sad when I wrote this]

I want things to matter as much to you as they do to me
I want to love and be loved equally

I never put your new name in my phone
Why would I change it?
I mean nothing is ever so much as in a name.
You're not his, to be honest,
not up to me to change
perception of what you show me,
you still treat me just the same.
So what's changed but your name?
Has It really? Be for real.
If there's nothing in a name it doesn't matter
***You're mine still.***

Apostrophe for ownership
Comma for the pause
I’m not sure if it’s a vow of spirit
Or just some papers and some laws.
What’s a paper to a poet?
What’s a spirit to a priest?
I’m writing in my temple
While you’re running through the streets.
Run to me ye’ faithful
Spill my wine like words so true
You’ll sleep next to the man who shows no love
***I’ll*** lay awake and ***dream of you.***

Do you enjoy being distant,
Or Indifferent?
A shame.
1,000 little kisses
New sounds within my name -
When it comes across your lips
I could have sworn you felt the same.

Maybe I am too impatient
Or I'm swerving from my lane.
Let me lie along the pavement
In a puddle
In the rain
Wash away my sins with whiskey
And my secrets just the same

I knew what this would bring
He who hesitates is lost
Found within the moment
I guess being blue's the cost.

My emotions shipwrecked seaside
On an island undisturbed.
I would build it back to hear you speak;
You haven't said a word.

If I'm not beside you
Then I'm on
***Do Not Disturb***

We ducked inside ***an alcove*** after being missed by rain all morning,
But it finally caught us.
I hugged you goodbye for the first time in forever.
We laughed.
I can remember the smell of the rain that begs the questions of the forthcoming summer.
The paint of the building blue, chipping, how many lovers had hidden in its presence before us?
The concrete seemed so sure of itself, the trees had a confidence I'd never seen before.
The rain fell harder and you looked up at me from your rightful place wrapped inside my arms.
For a moment the cars stopped, the rain froze, and time stood still.
All that was was your smile,
Your eyes,
Calling me long distance
And I'd pay the charge to answer them given the call again
Because your lips were on the line

I'd<br>
speak<br>
to you<br>
sweetly<br>
if only<br>
for a stolen<br>
moment on the<br>
stoop in Wasena<br>
hiding from the rain.

How ***do*** I explain
Wishing that this Xanax
Was cocain
Listening to Coltrane
Feeling like Cobaine
No Love
Tryinna show you my brain
Living on blue pack
American spirits
Bottles of champagne
“Capitalism sucks”
iWrite on my iMac
Complain
Come play
Songs you hear and think of me
If ***you*** even ***think of me***
(***at all***)

I want to be loved from that soft place that exists inside someone's heart. I want that place to be held for me. I want to feel their love coming from the corners they've left vacant, waiting to fill. I don't want to be a passing thought that comes and goes like undulating waves, I want to be the thought that rises, swells, and crashes into the shore: Constant, incessant, sure. I want the places that you hide to sound like my name if you tried to describe them.

I try to love from these places when I do love. I do love. I do, love.

I want to love you from the cobweb corners that no "could have beens, should have beens" have touched.

I want to fill the empty places in your heart with the love you deserve.

I hope that you ***love me just as much.***

Take the walls around the city tear them down to
have you with me

***jericho lover***

How did your lips cause me to write songs that made stars move but your distance has me calling on the galaxy to fold up?

You want the world,
But that belongs to some other girl,
Who's man still believes that he can change it.
There's other planets out there, dear,
So pick one and we'll claim it.
I'll crawl until I reach it,
Bring it back, and let you name it.

We can play pretend, that we're God and His Woman
I mean, in their images, we were made.
We can choose to hang the sun in a way that never sets,
And choose trees that will always give us shade.

We can color the seas the same color of your eyes,
So when you go walking and I stay behind,
Every time the waves wash ashore, they look at me so kind.

We can build a place that feels like home,
Big enough for us to roam,
Build a house, a bed, a throne,
And rule it as we always wished we could.

On our world there is no time,
Just your little hand in mine,
And songs we choose to sing a bit off key.

I'm sure we'll have to pick a center,
An orbit, that's your decision,
For all I know is ***you're the sun to me.***

I know you're mine.
What's meant for me is mine, I know,
And I've known you for a long time.

***clearly I know nothing***

Sometimes I lay wide awake at night wanting to tell someone that I'm sad. I want to express my pain to someone and I want them to understand.

I feel as if I have no one to tell. I can't tell the person I want to, or the people I want to, for a myriad of reasons. They wouldn't listen. Maybe I misjudge them and they would be all ears. Maybe this is the first projection because I won't listen to myself.

The issue is, no one ever seems to understand the way I'd like them to; their responses don't seem adequate. That's no fault of their own, this is my own reflection. The second projection.

I cannot figure out how to explain what I'm feeling. I can't express this lonely emptiness that permeates my mind. So how can I expect anyone else to understand it? I feel full at times, but this fullness comes from others. When I really have to sit with myself, be alone, be quiet, I feel empty inside. I do so much self care and self work. The "healing" journey and practice we all seem to be on now. I make great strides- literally and figuratively- but always feel I'm a step too short.

So often, I feel too inadequate to be loved. Am I Loved? Yes, but I rarely draw from a well I want to drink from. Not all love offered to you is meant for you. Subsequently, I suppose, not all love you desire is meant for you either. Maybe that's not my well because it's actually a puddle, and not my well because it's a stream that keeps moving. Maybe my well will be revealed when it's someone I can pour into who pours back in to me. At some point I've lost this analogy of the well, stream, or basin, or puddle, or

half empty glass, but the point is that love will be reciprocated when I know I've found my source. One day I won't be the only one pouring.
Regardless, I lay awake thinking of things I want to say to express this emptiness I feel, and my well feels dry. My bed feels cold. My arms would be better with someone in them. And I close my eyes and try to not feel so alone as I hold myself and go to sleep the most alone I've ever been.
***I try***, and like expressing the way I feel sad or someone understanding the depth that I mean, ***I fail.***

She whittled away at our communication, like wood verses the chisel. Tearing away at our connection slowly, a tap of metal with the lack of every syllable. We live in a time with 4 lines of communication, minimum, used to show someone that you're into them. 20 snaps a day drop to 10, to 5, to 1. Instagram story replies - to likes - to seen. The DMs that were sent of things you saw and thought of me turned to a like on 1 of 3 I sent when I thought of you, when originally you replied "that's cute" to at least a few. Now they're opened without a word from you.

The texts turn from paragraphs to sentences to syllables without periods. From all day, in the beginning until bed in the evening back to the beginning again, to once, if that, and then read.

How unfortunate we are to live in the easiest time of communication because it becomes perfectly apparent when someone doesn't want to speak to you.

***[congrats, you've been ghosted]***

I sit beside my car caught on the tire that blew out as I was driving. The vehicle held up by blown rubber and rusty old metal. A broken, bent jack lays cripple still clinging to the frame. Luckily, the axel is off the ground.

Cars, trucks, tractor trailers wiz past me. Busses, vans, and work trucks. 2 hours I've been stuck here, hazards flashing, and no one has stopped to lend a hand.

People often move over for police officers or 18wheelers in the shoulder, cops have passed in the adjacent lane.

Wolf spiders and grass hoppers in the Carolina grass have been more assistance to me than a passing man. We're the land of the free and the brave and the hospitable - hardly. Where is the southern charm and community? Where is the Christian passing me by answering the call or the Good Samaritan from the Rabi's teachings? I've seen three schools worth of fish decals. The Buddhist, Hindu and Muslim the same.

Where's the call to help our neighbor? A stranger? We live in fear and keep to ourselves. I can't even call the police, I'll be killed pulling my phone from my belt.

Beside The ***Unamerican Highway*** I sit, 85 heading north to Charlotte. A car I inherited from father resting on a tire that popped two exits back, wondering what the point of all of this is. I called out to God and found calm, then the jack broke and the car rolled. I sit on a spare that I hope isn't flat, when someone comes to help me fix it, I'll know.

The thoughts of existing no longer begin to creep in.
How complex that sentiment based on your perspective.
I long to no longer exist. Nothing seems to fit.
I hate ***every ounce of this.***

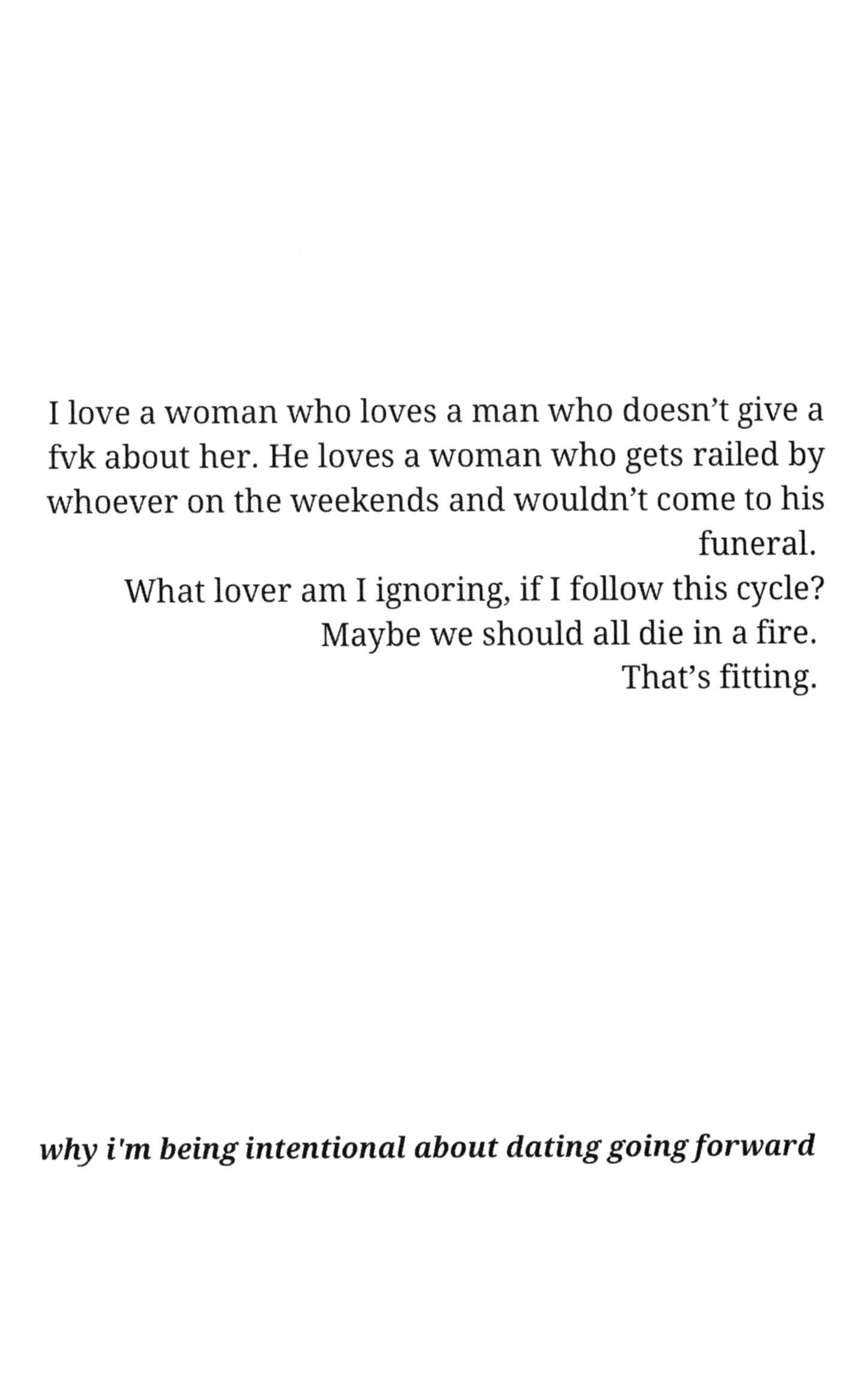

I love a woman who loves a man who doesn't give a fvk about her. He loves a woman who gets railed by whoever on the weekends and wouldn't come to his funeral.

What lover am I ignoring, if I follow this cycle?

Maybe we should all die in a fire.

That's fitting.

***why i'm being intentional about dating going forward***

Fvck you.
Look at you.
You sad piece of shit.
Hollow shell of what you should have been.
How dare you think that this would work?
The fear was somebody getting hurt and a tough situation becoming worse. So you were tender. You were sweet. You were kind. Why? You should have known that wouldn't work. Fvck her and ignore her like everyone else. Pretend friends, no feelings, no nostalgia, no longing. You dumb fvck. Why would you show anyone you cared? You know that's scary. To feel. To admit that the stolen glances are real. To acknowledge the spark between touches or the sensation when you kiss. You fool. You fvcking fool.
Fvck her and don't call for a month.
That's what they want.
No one wants a poem from a lover.
They want to be ignored by someone who doesn't love them.
Kill yourself. Maybe then they'll feel something.

*okay.*
***Conversations with the mirror at the bathroom in ikea.***

you have to hang in there
it gets better
we’ll get better
and one day
all the pain
will be worth it

***i promise***

I am dye-cast American dreams streamed out over midwestern telephone lines - your voice is the silence the radio man dreams of.

I'm rolled up $20 bills and swapping stories and sharing swim trunks and peanut m&ms with Hemingways.

My father lives in my little moments and poetry. He is an ever present part of me. I know he's proud of me.

I am the label peeled off of miller lite bottles as my society brother encourages my quasi-destructive yet ever entertaining bachelor antics. It's clear when he smiles that his fiancé loves him, she has the presence of an angel- a saint.

I'm a year and one month estranged from 30. I am ready, willing, and eager to carry forth this mantle of adventure into the era that others have described as a cemetery. Write my obituary in braille so that only the real can feel it. Write my will in pig Latin, sign it, seal it, and burry it beneath the field where I had my first kiss.

It's been 15 years since I knew a feeling like this.
I am tangled up wires and crisscrossed chords.
I'm an octave below the angels, I'm the New River Gorge.

How many candles were on my cake the year I learned I'd rather spend my birthday alone, hidden behind my parents bed beside the dresser, my two favorite toys and my imaginary friend beside me. 20 minutes they searched and couldn't find me. I remember my father's relief when he saw me, happy, smiling, picked me up and held me. It was too loud and too many people wanted to talk to me. For the rest of the day he held me.

Sometimes it's too much and there's no one here to hold me.

I am the boy who cries on his birthday. I am storm clouds following you down the west Florida coast. I am the boy running looking for sunshine.
I am sand in your frozen rum runner at Frenchy's.

I am the love you've always needed but you still can't see it clearly.
I'm the sound you make when you're alone and something touches you deeply.
I am the moment of epiphany spread out over a century.

I am the culmination of everyone who believed in me -
there is miraculous talent in my corner.

I am but a reflection of the great man that I'm becoming.

I am something.

I am nothing.

***I am.***

[redacted] 4:15 am

Going to bed when you hear the black birds:
***lovers and laborers alike***

Toe ring queen of teenage dreams
American spirit poolside romance
Backseat lover come closer, come over
The bridge, the parking lot calling

Blue ridge parkway blue light evading
Sunrise creeping through the trees
Hands on trembling knees
Learning that you kiss like me

We were 18, 28, 33
Kiss and dance our bones collide
Notch the list finish another
Have we felt the same ***all this time***?

greg bradies, hopping fences
could you be my summer princess?
kiss me like i've kissed the shore a thousand times before.
nail me down for when you're back, text me,
grab a drink and laugh.
i'm always on the road but what's home? Give me a call.
the first kiss taste of cigarettes then sharing one before we kissed, to you telling me we'd kissed between those two, you reminisce.
innocent and pure and sweet
promise, save a space for me. I'll sleep between you,
it's nothing
frank singing while I dodge the lights.

hold me on these summer nights,
sun coming up, windows cracked.
happy to help you feel again,
***my angel in the back*.**

You speak of liberation, finding yourself. And I see that brightness in your eyes.
You've got a growing sense of worth, of who you are, and why.
It's beautiful beside you. You tell me you love the first moment in the beginning, penetration, learning more.
You love that I'm vocal; I tell you what I'm thinking.
I hope you're thinking of me.
Sharing space is special; you and I shared the same space briefly.
***I'll come home*** again
***To see you*** soon
Hoping you feel the way you did back then.

To strip these vices from my fingers:
Blank slate, clean sheets, fresh snow.

To know that what I deserve exists;
To know you're mine and that's it.

***to find what i'm looking for***

Maybe it's us when it's said and done
Maybe it's you beside me
Maybe I'll find the love I'm looking for
***Maybe it's*** inside ***me***

Sometimes I want to go home.
I'm growing weary before I'm growing old.
A meadow of green grass with a large willow in the middle,
tall, ample space beneath it.
Apple trees line the shallow valley,
a quaint creek runs crooked through the plain in a way that splits the space into thirds.
There's an old set of fence posts, still intact enough to give the illusion that the sides were once separated.
Beneath that tree standing tall, I lay in the middle,
Feeling small. I'm at the center of this universe
lounging in a place where nothing else matters.
In a time before beer, women, whiskey, and cigarettes, I'm content with apples, chocolate, and water.
I have my bag with books, a notepad, and a couple of toys just in case.
I'm 7, 11, 17: still green.
I'm in love with my innocence. I feel love swelling through me for nothing in particular.
I'm not with my family but I can feel them, I know they're well elsewhere, safe and healthy.
The sun shines down across the plain I'm in,
settling on trees that are dancing with the breeze rolling by.
Green foliage against the pale blue sky,
Fluffy white clouds in places mimic the green burst on top of long brown trunks,
In other places the clouds whisper out like white lines across an aqua colored mirror.

How I long to feel the feeling of the sun on my skin
before I knew it's impermanence.
I want to sleep on the brown and white blanket I
borrowed from my parents closet,
holding close to me my books and stuffed friends,
my back pack a pillow
I'd never have to lift my head again,
yet sleep peacefully, knowing fully,
***I was home,***
***And I was loved.***

I'll hide away this pain some day, trade it in for cards and candy
Cocktail hour laughs and glasses emptied early
Hands shaken shoulders touched cheeks kissed
Laughs and smiles and sighs and "yeah"
Subtle indicators I'm okay on the surface
Feeling deeper when I inhale and say "no really, I'm great."
One day I'll mean it, really, I will, believe me.
Have faith in me like a deity; Calgary salvation saving me.
*Have faith in me*
I'll hide away this pain some day
Impatiently: some day
***Just wait for me, okay?***

I wonder what I would look like loving you;
What you look like loving me?
Let's make an "us loving us"
documentary, ***if you're into me.***

I want the kind of love I dream and write about
Felt it in your hands at the coffee shop
Saw it your eyes when you opened up to me
Could almost taste it in your smile when you're close to me
Why do you hold it back?
He doesn't want it
He doesn't deserve it
Why am I locked out of heaven
How could I earn it
***If loving you was a language*** I'd learn it
But it seems I'm deaf to the sound of the lips that I long for

Today I slept in,
I ironed a shirt.
I went for a run.
I went to the gym.
I cooked breakfast at lunch time.
I opened a bottle of champagne because I had it
I toasted to the woman I met at the bar last night
She invited me back to her room after singing Katy Perry Karaoke
I bought drinks for the people who bring me drinks at the bar I go often
I was glad I left the house
I didn't drink too much
Today I ironed a shirt before I put it on
I cleaned my house
Today I toasted to something good
instead of drinking because most things aren't
Today I slept in.
Ironed my shirt.
I'm okay today,
I really am.

***a Sunday in march***

I had this thought of me and you renting a cheap motel/hotel on the outskirts of town. Maybe 30 or 45 minutes out just because I want to ride in the car with you.
I want to hold your hand.
I thought of us getting a bottle of Jack Daniels and ginger ale.
Taking a bluetooth speaker and creating a shared playlist called *nights when we don't exist*.
I thought of you and I dancing and laughing, jumping between the beds like two kids on their first vacation.
I'm thinking of you in your underwear and a blackish gray band t-shirt, laughing.
Your smile in the yellow hotel lamp lighting is heaven sampled for a few seconds.
I don't care if I never touch you, It's watching you dance and sing your songs,
Bottle in hand, standing beside the bed, that's filling me up.
I'm thinking of placing my head on your stomach as you stand between my legs and play with my hair.
How I'd love to wrap you up.
How I could stay in that moment for who knows how long.
How I'd love to lay with you.
Lay you down.
Or lay in the bed on the other side of the room and listen to an album until the covers touch
And time for us to crawl under the covers finally comes.
The thought of turning down the bed with you sends butterflies into my stomach;

The moment of crawling in next to you could send
me crawling into a hole,
But I feel whole simultaneously.
I want to put our phones in the drawer and forget
that they exist- but we need them for the music.
I need you for the music.
Oh how you're the song that I haven't written.
I want to write you out to the melody,
Lay your lines on the page and feel the way they feel
coming across my lips.
I'll recite them and practice them until they're
performance perfect
at which point I'll know your every inch.
I long to hold you like a beat, carry you like a tune,
sing your body song until you hum with me.
I want to get a pack of American Spirits, light blue,
and a baby blue lighter.
I want to sit on the balcony and share one or three
with you.
I want to put our last ones out on each other's arms;
my right and your left, while we hold hands.
So that one day, when we hold hands again,
You can see both of our scars side by side from the
night that doesn't exist.
I want to carry a piece of you with me. Forever.
Taste you every time I taste whiskey.
Feel you when my eyes get teary,
When everything is blurry I remember your smile
clearly.
Why is this only ***a made up memory?***

***Why cry over Augusta?***
I have Tampa, Prague, New York.
Richmond. Baltimore. Roanoke, of course.
Blacksburg, Boone, a couple cities way out West
Jacksonville, Savannah and Atlanta if I'm stressed.
Charlotte for a midway, Amsterdam is between
So how does an Augusta night in Athens
Feel like home to me?

I’d ***bleed a thousand pens*** for you if it would sail the ships
If words wouldn’t work to get you here
I’d open up my wrist

I hope you’re up there fishing, Dad,
Your son's still down here grieving
Looking for a wife and drinking whiskey in the evening.

I hope you’re up there fishing, Shawn,
I’m down here rambling, carrying on
Dreaming of the things you said you’d tell me when I’m older.

I know too many angels, to call them all by name
Just know when I’m awake
That they’re here within my brain.
They visit in my dreams, guide me through my days.
One day I’ll ask God
Why they couldn’t stay
***Face to face.***

I hope the skies are blue for you,
I hope the fish are biting.
Thanks for teaching me to read,
Introducing me to writing.

For the running shoes you gave me,
When you made them all that money,
For being a good dad to me,
Gabrielle, my friends, and Sonny.

Thanks for being humorous,
For laughing loud and true.
Thanks for standing in the gap for me,
For always coming through.

Thank you for that beer that night
In the hot tub in the smokies.
Thanks for making me pull up my jeans
Telling me black men don't wear croakies.

Thank you for the politics,
The whiskey, and the hugs.
Thanks for being kind to me,
***Dad***, thank you for the love.

Thank you for the poetry,
For all of your support.
***Thanks*** for how you molded me,
***For being you***, in short.

I can’t be patient enough
If my life was
What it should be
It would be
Vacant enough
I’m not grateful enough
I been hateful too much
Spend my time in a rush
All I’m needing is Love
Feel like that’s
Asking too much
I've been thinking too much
I've been drinking too much
**I'm not**
**present** enough

I find myself
out on the road
at a fishing hole
driving home
catching a peace of mind
a piece
of feeling whole

I struggle to express the depths at which I feel alone.
Loneliness amplified by the existence of our phones.
Communication easy as it's ever been for centuries
If you wanted to there's 1,000 ways you can reach me.

Read receipts, apologies of "I'm just bad at texting"
Bluetooth, wifi, phone lines, still we're disconnecting.
We're only just a call away until one day we're not.
The depth of my loneliness: the bottom of the plot.

***read, delivered, opened, seen***

I don't feel worth choosing.
I must not be, because if I were,
Someone would have done so.
Yet they haven't.
I'm here alone, so maybe it's me.
It's my fault. Maybe they
Don't know they can have me.
Maybe I'm just unwanted.
That pill is harder to swallow.
Maybe people have met me
And realized they'd rather have
Someone else. This goes for jobs,
Friendships, relationships.
Isolation is an understatement.
Why don't they want me back?
Am I not a commodity?
Is my life a comedy?
***What is wrong with me?***

I feel so alone when I fall asleep
I think of the nights you were next to me
I long to feel whole, home, and warm again
Praying God will bring me
Someone who doesn't leave me
***I fall asleep alone***

I am but a pawn in a chess game that I did not agree to play. I am on the front line, waiting, hoping to not be sacrificial, but rather, praying to be instrumental.

Playing instrumentals, rhyming in syncopation,<br>anticipation, placation my art of orderly<br>conversation.

Like the ***PlayStation***, gray box with strings attached
Chasing wild apes through jungles
I can't escape
I am solid around snakes, my gear metal
Raiding the tomb of the new devils
No jewels at new levels
I gotta crash to keep my new mask
Need for speed in life - give it more gas
Splintering my cells
Like stained glass
I am just a hit man creeping
On manicured grass
Sands of time leaking
No prince, you know that,
If you get me, then you get me,
Like references of a throwback

*I can still hear your laugh  no matter how much time has passed*

Coffee,
Sparkling water,
Champagne.
Cold showers,
Birthday indecision,
A book about writing.
Poetry.
Succession.
Open window,
Zoom call conversations.
Thoughts of you,
Texts unread,
Lack of hesitation.
Water bottles,
Cups of quarters,
Zillow searches,
Job applications.
Gym sessions,
Stretch marks,
Night swims,
First kisses for the 3rd time.
Therapy sessions,
Cafe lunches,
Brand new numbers.
Flat tires,
Casual dates,
Crushes,
Crushes on the
Top golf waitress.
Weddings.
Reservations,
Champagne sent
As birthday wishes,
House music,
Jazz,
Rap,
Poetry.
***This is summer.***

July 8th, 2023

You made it. Another year around the sun. I pray for our sake that you feel better tomorrow than you did a year ago. That day kind of set the tone for this year, didn't it? But that's okay. These dark days, weeks, months and maybe years can prove as a juxtaposition for the days that are shining bright. I feel a bunch of those in our future. I'm proud of you, no matter what that voice in our head says, and I'm glad we're still here.

The truth is that this is the end of a decade of tough moments, of pain, and loss. This is our last chapter to close this book triumphantly, and we will do that. The lessons of perseverance, grace, achievement and understanding purpose cannot be understated. We are great and meant for great things. Great things are coming to us because we are already great and we attract what we are. We are deserving, determined, and destined.

That's the theme for 29. The set up for the most successful 30s the world has ever seen.

I love you.

I'm proud of you.

Happy Birthday Eve, Tyler.

***Love,***
***Yourself.***

Your

love

is

like

my

words

off

of

six

teq
uilas

*all over the place*

July 14

I am very much aware that I am alive
Hopping into a metal tube, sat between two strangers, to go 784 miles through the air to see my friends from college in a city where the buildings cut thru the skies.

A man beside me sleeps with sports center playing to his closed eyelids like my uncle did on afternoons when he was off from his job at the medical center, sleeping in the small apartment we shared in Salem, Virginia.

The woman to my right closed the window and scrolls movies on her seat back TV, unable to make a decision of what to watch as I can't decide who I want to be.

My friends are celebrating the idea that our friend has found someone to love him equally and involve the law and the Lord in their decision to share space and time until they either can't or don't want to anymore. We're going to watch baseball and eat Italian food, drinking pilsners and smoking filtered cigarettes, celebrating the end of of his singleness as the dying American youth that we are.

The city grows through the now cracked window as we descend through the turbulence due to the heat.

This summer is hotter than a summer has ever been: a scientific fact.

The streets will push that heat back up towards me as I walk through the screaming corridors fighting to pull my dreams back to the surface while being mindful of the moment and grateful that I get to exist in a time as easy as this. If I know anything, it's that things get harder as we go, and maybe it won't be this easy again. What's holding me back? What's holding me down?

The heat hasn't changed me, the wheels touch the tarmac, and I'll be waiting for an Uber, an elevator, a beer, a ride home, a flight back south, and for truth to come to the surface again in no time.

Three weeks ago I felt like no one loved me. My life is full of love at this moment. Women waiting on me to visit their cities, to come home, to come to my senses.

I feel everything and nothing all at once.

July 21

I feel as if my purpose eludes me. Rain falls on the concrete outside my apartment as thunder claps in the skies and lightening brightens the room only for a second, the way the smile from a girl you're fond of does your life - only for a second. The long, loud booms of thunder and brief flashes of lightening,

In my feverish state for a moment I feel peaceful.

I wish I could go home again.

My home no longer exists. It's now a 4/2 on a corner lot that sold for twice it's equity after an auction where it was bought for a fourth of what it was worth.

The world is cold and lonely.

I'm cold and lonely,

but ***I'm not the world.***

All of it's so draining
Drift off to nothing
I need something
Make me feel
Make me real
Make me
Something

***make me***

Posted Pictures
Birthday at the beach
The man
Smiling beside you
Should be
Me

***July 20 Something***

one day
i’ll die &
GOD will
show me
how to
do it
all right
***next time***

Maybe in my next
life
I won’t feel so
***a l o n e***

***Movies are cool.***
For a moment, or collection of moments, we don't have to exist. We can completely detach from reality and peer into somewhere else, through a new perspective, and exist without space and time. We are able to remove ourselves from the fabric of this reality and tether ourselves to film reels rolling through another. If the movie is good, we are able to realize our potential in another form, a transcendent state, a new paradigm. Films allow us to live other lives without completely leaving this one behind. And what a blessed time for us to exist, a movie about dolls and a movie about bombs, fantasy and factual horror, patriarchy and purpose. To be fully immersed in either a rich blessing, moving beyond the bounds of our existence, if only for an afternoon, to experience the blissful embrace that is cinema.

Until one day
It's my turn
To be the one
Undeserving

***unevenly yoked***

That summer we rode around with our tanks on E
15 here, 20 there, 11.11 every now and again
Low fuel and little orange gas tank lights reminders of the slowing economy
The hottest summer on record for the 5th time in our lives now,
A headline we will learn to live with.
How we've had fun with the windows down,
Singing songs we find through apps by artists on failing tours
Switching from champagne with yellow labels to brands of the grocery stores
I'm still punching above my weight, living above my means
Double features of movies of dolls and bomb makers
Liberation and detonation a theme of social life in 23
watch billionaires on TV and talk to millionaires at lunch
As the waitress runs my card and I hope I'm not over my limit too much
Not how I saw the age at which I've arrived
But I supposed I'm grateful I'm alive
We'll remember this summer in the American Heat, spurred hotter by Canadian Smoke
When our phone batteries were always low
Homelessness was at an all time high
But more and more jobs were made by the day.
We'll remember this summer in the American Heat,
The first of a dying decade
A dying summer
A setting sun
Until it's ***summer no more***

Open my mind to anything
Let a little too much light in
Growing thin
***I need to learn boundaries***

I'll spend

my summers

forever jealous

of the sun that gets

to kiss your skin

***the girl at Kure Beach***

I told you forever when we were 13
and
what if I meant it?

What if
that love
lingers
'til
we’re
ghosts?

Does it matter
that there’s others
who now
hold places
we first
explored
together?

Or in the continuum of space and time
Are we forever together tethered
even if you aren't still mine?

***notes from middle school eternal***

Miller lite
Crown- on the rocks
Connecting me
To my father and brother
In spirits

***the usual after a long day***

*aka "The Recipe"*

Holding hands in Normaltown, laughing
Walking 'round trees fallen down
Posing for pictures, laughing
First kisses over first espresso martinis
Laughing,
Throwing darts and talking, laughing
Meeting for margaritas and secrets
Settling for a garage that offers seating,
Laughing, drinking
And to think
You were standing me up
Until we were meeting
And laughing
Talking, drinking,
And ***laughing***

You've been on my mind since you left
Standing in the kitchen wearing my blazer
Drinking espresso like it's life's elixir
Kissing me goodbye like you were leaving for work
I cleaned the room as if
**You were** coming **home** again

I’ll live my life safer, a tad bit more pure
Keep my spot free for me
by my dad on the shore.

***a pledge & a prayer***

Sometimes
I think it should be
Little Lee, Sonny, and Me
Fishing on a bank
Basking in the sun.

Shooting the breeze
As it blows thru the trees
Talking to my Father, Haywood and Shawn
While Fatman and Heidi are egging us on.

Waiting on supper cooked by my grandmother
Who dances in a kitchen with women who love her,
Who prays for the women still waiting to join her.

I think of the days where I shouldn't have made it
I wonder who prayed it,
Who's keeping me here?

I feel like a failure,
Not fit for The Savior,
Who's rescued me year after year after year.

They're not here now,
They're there in the clouds,
I'll keep on working on making them proud.
So quiet my thunder,
Answer my wonder,

and ***tell me how to live without*** all of ***you*** now.

Take me down to
New Amsterdam
Stand along the water
Write our names on walls
The lips of a new lover
Daughter, sister, mother
Become one with the moment
Retrace. Rinse. Repeat.
Call to me on a tune
Hold me forever
In the stories you'll tell
Of ***times you're glad you had***.

When the
Voice inside
Your head
Sneezes,
Do you
Tell it
God bless you?

**August 3rd, 4:45 AM**

I feel sick thinking of my life that is leaving me. I feel sick not making it to my friends wedding in California. I feel alone and left out. Abandoned by my dreams and by myself. Forgotten by life, God, and success because I'm in debt and I can't afford a weekend away. For the first time in my life I said it's smarter not to travel, not to go. "What if I don't have it?" And for the first time I don't have it. And I hate it. I've never listened to the voice of lack but I have and now

I feel like nothing and I fear I have nothing. I hate this place. I never wanted to be here. I am drowning. I am doing my best to swim, fighting the current, I am treading water refusing to sink and go under. I have worked myself up and woken myself up in the middle of the night. Sweating, cursing, tossing and turning, feeling as if I'm going insane.

I am doing my best to convince myself it's fine. Things happen as they should. Things are what they should be but it feels like a lie. It feels like I'm lying to myself and I know it. Lying in my own faith. I feel removed from the flow, from life, from God, from being where I am meant to be. And I know that's not true. But it feels true. And it brings me immense pain.

I haven't felt this pain before. The way I do. But I'm going to battle it sober. No alcohol. No porn. No sex. No addictions to cover the pain of this existence. But the pain is real and it is raw. Grief is beneath the surface like a rash festering in this summer heat begging to be felt and I am refusing to scratch it- but I must. I need to open the wounds, clean them out, sew them up. And move on.

I want my life to be different. I want my story to be different. And I must author that future by dedication, intention, and deliberate action today. I'm so tired of being tired and sad and broke. God please give me a better life.

**August 3rd, 4:45 AM**

*I feel like everyone is passing me by*
*I'll fade away*
*And no one will notice*

I am a lamp post
Tall, and green.
yellow bulb atop of me.
My light is starting to dim.
It will fade, and flicker
Burn bright
Then extinguish
    And no one will notice
Back and forth
They continue walking
I'm left standing
In isolated darkness

***bright but dying alone***

I feel the time of my life
Casually passing away
Before my eyes

I too, am passing away
In pieces at a time

As if I can do nothing
To stop ***the bleeding***
***Of my youth***

Someone has to sit around
Sip the coffee, tea
Smoke the cigarettes
Sleep
Do nothing.
Someone has to
Or else
Who would we
Aspire to be?

***the grindset is overrated***

The cicadas in the morning
Are the southern sound
Of summer Sundays
Heating up

and i'm happy to hear them
from ***within your arms***

*A series of poems:*

# *"To california:*

## *if only I had gone"*

On a flight over America, LAX bound, I sip from my gin and tonic and question what it means to be
“In Love.”
Will I ever know Love again or is it a fleeting, failing concept that I’m doomed to study and analyze but never realize for myself?
Is Love finite, meaning only a certain number of us experience it in this existence or is it infinite, meaning there’s enough of it for everyone to experience, however, not all of us encounter it? Has the market placed a limit on it the way we’ve done with food distribution? Is there enough love to go around, ending world hunger, but love isn’t grown to feed, it’s grown for profit? Do people only offer love when there’s something to be gained? No one loves for Love’s sake?

"another drink, sir?"

***yes*** and one of those cookies, ***please***.

Another gin and tonic, America expands outside my window beneath the clouds.

oh, if there is love, can I have it now as well, please?

Backyard garden waltz
Champagne toast
Romance
Coast to Coast
Love eternal
Like the waves
Along a rocky
California shore

***I really love weddings***

I am not a scientist.
I am awake on the floor.
The land of sunshine has,
And always will,
Call me to it's coasts.
I am but a stranger;
Dreamer, writer,
Wandering lover.
Invited, not included
Introduced, and thought of later.
I am not a doctor,
I am not a lawyer.
I am good at conversation,
Eye contact, giving speeches.
I am decent at listening,
Not the best at remembering,
But I'm good at kissing,
Drinking, and being a gentleman.
I am not a physicist, an executive,
Or an associate at a firm.
I am a writer, a friend,
Lover. I am a brother.
I am an artist.
I am sorry I wasn't at your wedding.
***The two of you***
***Looked lovely***.

It’s wild to know your friends in college
Apple cores and piles of books
Sleeping on Sweet Briar floors
Smoking on the president’s porch
To seeing them in suits and tuxedos
Walking down the isle to get married
Knowing now what we didn’t know then
Watching our youth grow thin
Yet simultaneously
Feeling ***the youngest we’ve ever been***

end collection

***

back to the muddled mix of poetry

Play pretend
"New partner"
Phone face down
Kissing night stand
Play Pretend
"New Lover"
Syncing playlists
Syncing nights end
Like we spend
Days and days
Together
Your day concludes
Mine does too
Attempt sleep
Toss turn
Breathe think
I should write
***A letter from***
***your latest lover***
***on sleepless***
***nights***
to you.

Would your love for me persist
If I told you
***my darkest truths?***

Sometimes I wonder if any of the fish my father and I caught are still living,
Swimming, grateful we let them go.
Waiting to be another father-son duo's memories of Summer Sunday's fishing
***Catch and release.***

I think of you in aisles of the craft store
Full of potential creative energy
Projects and hobbies and Saturdays worth
Of things to do
I see all of the pieces needed to make something beautiful
And ***I think of you***

Do
you
ever
ask God
how
His
day
is
going?

Time is rubber in the summer
On nights with stems and caps
And tassels and speakers
Australian singers and cauliflower crusts

***caps, cats, and the color of heat***

These South West Virginia roads wind and make me feel at home.
The Blue Ridge Mountains hold my soul.
The skies hang in shades of blue that know the days of the boy I've been.
Oranges, pinks, and purples splash across the sky on summer nights before darkness falls like silence over the valleys and the stars hang as if only hung for Roanoke.
The foliage in the fall is Hokie maroon, orange, crimson, lining the highways from Abington to Arlington. Williamsburg to Farmville, Virginia Beach to Lexington.
The air fresher than you've ever known, lungs filling with generations of hope and love and the belief that things can always and *will always* get better.
Sundays spent in services hearing sermons, laughing on porches with loved ones, living for a moment in a moment when the second hand was a few seconds slower.
Home is laughing with my uncles in the kitchen at 2 am; Walking in Wasena, Grandin; running in Raleigh Court and Salem, sleeping in south county, creating off of Fairhope and Cove, Electric, Apperson, Pin Oak.
It's beer in Lee-Hi Lanes,
Greg Bradys at Jack Browns,
2 hots without and a Travis at Texas Tavern.
It's Something in the Water
It's the sky over the rolling hills of Sydney
Downtown nights in Richmond
The people who say they miss me
The friends who say they get me.
It's the mountains,
The air,
***The Commonwealth,***
***Within me.***

I should have loved you when I knew you
You were cake
And all I wanted to do was starve
To drown
I would gladly be a fat kid if I met you now
-word to Curtis Jackson

***wish i had never wanted ice cream***

I can't fold the pieces in        I try until it's all nothing.
Mangled mess, scraps, and parts of something that could have been                                        but wasn't.
I walk along the highway        Open Road Holy Solace, seeking shelter thinking praying wishing

All but working    Becoming

Practicing    Being

Would you believe me if I told you ***every secret***? What if there were words to describe the color of the sunset on the day your father died? Can I paint for you a picture                        or are you also color blind?

The days are long when you're not drinking.
There's no break from yesterday to today to tomorrow. No hard stop. Sleep is better, and it's deeper. Richer. There's no mental laps between events, no break or change in consciousness. I felt it briefly, in a kiss, an escape, but that's different than the bourbon and beer. I see things clearly, without the whiskey.
**Days are different when you're not drinking.**

I live my life where my weeks don't have real Fridays
I end my weeks on Thursdays, start on Wednesdays,
But I always rest on Sundays.
My weeks are strung together like string lights
Over a small cafe on a terrace;
Calm, bright, bustling at times,
Moments of flashes and dark spots.
My life is one long week that cycles in and out.
All days have meaning and some mean nothing.
The concept of Monday and Friday need not apply.
Every day is beautiful, every day is nothing;
But Tuesdays?
***I love Tuesdays*** the most.

Standing outside
Throwing clouds into the sky
Could I be God for the weekend?
Create a new existence,
Sinews of perception
Could I
Hold All creation in my hands
And not crumble?

***could i be God for the weekend?***

If you’re a wallflower, I long to be paint

To the girls with cool tattoos who love Mac Miller's
music and making out:

You're angels amongst mortals
there's a special place for you
In Heaven
In my heart
Anywhere I spend time

***45s and wine***

I saw the color blue and thought of you

***a poem in 9 words***

How easy to be pretty,
Blameless, blemish free
American Beauty
Extra Fare
Open Sea

To be the brightened smile
With light behind her eyes
What is this life
If not a ***daydream with you***

When do scarlet flags turn beige then cream?
Colors run
Red flag dream
You kiss like love was real
I surrender;
***War no more within me***

I’ll miss you the way
                                        The leaves miss the trees;
                                        The trees miss their leaves.
In spring
Color me green,
Bloom;
Love me,
Summer;
Fall,
Leave me again.
***this winter may be a little colder***

Play pretend: I'm God
Beg you be Sky
Paint colors across your canvas
**Creation in your eyes**

One day we all go home
Great Awakening
Call me up
Send me off sweetly
Hug my mother & sister if they're here
Pour beer and whiskey for my sons
Give wine and roses to my daughters
Make a dinner for their mother
Or say something kind to a stranger
If it's simply just me
***As it always has been***

Tank on E down Timothy
Take Care, The Ride there
I'm here
The West Side Winterville
Summer cold still sweating
Dressed in sweats
I keep my hat on inside
Tea in a kettle
White gown white flag waving
Sheets like an oasis
Homeostasis attempted
Four of Wands pulled before me
Yellow kitchen homecoming
Celebration of sobriety
Little lights from Thai Land flicker
Roommates bicker
Parisian princess reading poetry
A moment
Everything is perfect
A moment
The moon is halved
I'm whole
***[how you beside me feels like home]***

The second person in the bed exacerbates the
brokenness, right? Like when you're alone
you don't notice it?

***because you sleep in the middle***

I think of you when you’re not around
My bed feels fuller with you in it
It’s your smile that’s made me enjoy this town
I said ***I appreciate you***, and I meant it

***if it weren't for distance, would we be lovers?***

Afternoons feel better
Holding your hand
Coffee and lemonade
Mix
Riding while playing
Frank
Sleeping in, talking
Late
I love to
Hear what you
Think

***struck match***

Though it hurts that I feel that it's all that I'll be
I'm glad
You call me your friend

***if that's all you ever call me***

The smell of grass from your childhood home is lost
until you're on an old back road
Missing those that are dead and gone
And they remind you
You're close to home
Through the fresh cut blades
On the end of an August Breeze
As a country song plays
And summer
Starts to fade

***windows down in winder***

I thought it would have happened when I woke up covered in the night before,
But it didn't.
When I barely missed a DUI for God knows what reason, pulled over off of 15, allowed to drive back to the U.
I thought it would have happened when I messed up the job interview;
When I called my sister screaming, crying, cussing,
But it didn't.
It happened when I was running
And realized my life would be better sober
That Sundays are nice when I'm not hungover
It happened slowly
Then all at once
And the cold bois and cocaine quit calling so often
The calls soften
Until NA beers are better than AA peers
And the only cold boys
Are me and the homies outside laughing

***you grow up when you're ready***

Are all epiphanies meant to be shared or are some sacred?

Dear ████

I wish we were still the friends we should have been. Could have been- had I not tried to love you as a boy, stepped back, and been the honest man I wanted to be.
I apologize for my father's advice, I think he tried to do his best by me. Still, I could have loved you differently.
If we were the friends we'd talk about how fair or unfair these years have been. I'll forever appreciate you and your father's visit when my father was leaving. Even after everything you were there when it was a friend I was needing. I still remember the Bahamas trip I promised your mother, when the two of you believed in me like no other. Maybe we'd discuss the love we've found or lost in others. Your boy next door is marrying the girl who broke my heart in 2019. Maybe that's the long arm of karma coming to strike me for the three summers he watched us fall in love, scraping our knees, up and down the cul-de-sac of your childhood street. I've come to learn things are as they should be - or call it faith as it could be - and I do my best to believe that's true. I've come to learn that there are pieces of me that only exist because of you. I met a man who knows the man you're going to marry - he told me about y'alls first date after I told him you were my high school sweetheart. Weird information for him to give me, I thought, but what do I know. I have a job that's not paying me enough, nothing really, and I feel like I'm always behind the eight ball lately.

I think often of my jeep, parking at the end of the street, and holding your hand. I miss laughing with you in English class.

I've come to learn that time isn't exactly linear, so in some timeline, we're perpetually laughing about our crushes, before we ever kissed, and maybe as that timeline expands we're talking about new ideas of love, places we want to visit, and our desire to learn French.
Who knows what it all means in the end, but I wish you were still my friend.

I'll think of you often, until I'm no longer, and somewhere in my writing your friendship will always exist.

***Sincerely yours*** almost forever,

Tyler James

I want to love on purpose
Provide support and comfort
Coffee in the morning,
Flowers in the afternoon,
Dinner in the evening
Comfort when we sleep

You fit beside me
You kiss like me
But not just like me

I want to love you on purpose
I crave you with intention
I want to give what you deserve
I want to love with your permission

***to whomever, whenever the time comes***

To kiss between your shoulder blades where your wings should be

I want to know that everything is okay.
I want to look at my account
And sigh a sigh of relief
I want to know I can help anyone
I want to know that space and time and I exist
Peacefully
I want to travel and eat and drink
And breathe
Peacefully
I want to know that my loved ones are fine
Happy, at home, warm, and fed
I want to sleep and dream and think
***Peacefully***

Laugh, kiss me
I won't call you "lover"
Hold me, touch me,
Move closer, back to sleep
Mix of imported coffees
Cuddled on the couch
How to start the day as peacefully
As humanly possible

***a morning that happened once***

Some are stressed,
Hands on foreheads pressed
Some laugh and text
Some work in small circles
 Some alone
Some sit around a table as if on a sitcom
They laugh louder than they talk
Some queue in line
Some pace on the phone
A couple reads books,
 She has an ankle tattoo of the Crucifix
 Obviously gotten to show faith and
 Solidarity with her tattooed grandkids
A man in a headband eats egg bites
 watching videos loudly on his phone
The paired and solo people working
All look content or lonely
I sit and I watch and I write
***People in the coffee shop***

One day in Paris I'll step out on a balcony
Light my cigarette
think of you
Wonder if you've seen this view
And ask.
I'll laugh
And know that you're nearby

One day in Prague I'll step out on a balcony
Light one, take a sip of coffee
think of all the days I spent so sad
I'll wonder if I'm better now
I'll laugh
And know that good times lay ahead

One day in Roanoke I'll step out on my patio
And have a sip of tea.
I'll look out over the yard
think of all that they will be
I'll wonder if you've seen this view
I'll smile and I'll l think of you
I'll laugh
And know you see it too

***life could be so scenic***

For the first time in my life
  It's hard to pay my bills
But what really matters?
I wake up tomorrow anyway.
Landlord, tax man, debt collectors
Will be okay.
The saddest part is knowing
None of this is necessary
We have more than enough
To leave, experience, breathe, be
  Freely
But you'd rather me be broke
And bummed out about it
So you can have your pennies

What's a million worth
If you can't enjoy your moments?
You're so afraid of losing yours
You can't let me keep mine,
Can you?

***"i'm an acquisitions manager"***

I’ve never loved waking up
as much as I do
next to you

***to whomever, whenever the time comes pt 2***

To love something wild is terrifying;
Terrific.
To know that they're not yours for long
Is a passion worth lamenting.

***and given the chance i'd try again***

Notifications not meant for you
Reminders of what it is
what it isn't
Messages to calm the storm
Before the rage
Whispers you away

***privacy screens should be stock features***

Take me to your hidden garden
I'll pretend I've never seen it
Sunken secrets
Kiss me sober

***seltzer water cheers***

I should be bar hopping in New York, falling for a stranger I’ve only just met.

***That’s it.***
***That’s the poem***.

I can taste that you're just for me
Kissing across your thighs
You feel like the first time
For the 5th time as the night becomes morning

And I'm wrong
On so many levels
And I'm gone
As sober as I've been
As over as I've ever been

and I'm gone

***how i wish it could be different***

Whenever I'm sick I'm somehow always reminded of how much I hate capitalism. It's September 6th, I've been sick since the 1st with some bacterial infection the doctors can't pinpoint. At the doctor's office I had an icee popsicle thing, the one from our childhood, and it's the first thing I've been able to "eat" in a week. I need some for the house and I've set out on a mission to buy them. Every store says "sorry, that's a seasonal item" Labor Day was Monday... this is Wednesday. You're telling me the entire stock is just GONE now? Also, summer ends the 21st, when the seasons change. We're so in a rush to move from one thing to the next and it makes me sick. we haven't had the equinox and I'm seeing pumpkin decorations in full force in all of the aisles; the leaves haven't changed. We rush from one quarter to the next with quotas and profits and losses. I wish we cared more about people, experiences, and when the actual seasons changed. Yes, this is because we're out of icees, but there's a deeper meaning than that

I wish I was at my Uncle William's house who had a fridge in the garage full of icee pops.
***I wish our system was different.***

I'm not making six figures
But I'm loving people like you taught me

I'm not selling a million records
But I'm on the records talking

You can't find me on the shelf
But I'm finding myself within the writing

I'm not the man I wanted to be, *yet,*
But I'm kind, intentional, and honest

***The way you raised me.***

*The hungover Sunday in Manhattan*
*I passed so many people I felt I couldn't help*
*This was merely a reflection showing me*
***I couldn't help myself***

I wrote this poem
On a napkin
Tucked it in a jacket in Nantucket
    You said you loved it.
I held your hand and stood beside you
                    out in public
For the first time    in a long time
I knew that I could trust it.

I wrote this poem
Just to tell you
I've always felt free    in your presence.
The way your eyes    are surely blue
Is the way            I'm sure of you
***I wouldn't change a single thing for a second***

extra poems
just for you
because you bought this
book before anyone
else knew who I was

**9/16/23 4:07 am**

I will make my life better.
The best part is coming next.

I am building, manifesting,
and accepting the amazing
things that are happening to
and for me.

**12:57 am mon sept 18**

Sing sweet like alter songs,
Swing low, call me home
Spit cherrie pits, tie knots in cherry stems
Kiss me, summer fades away
Memories are made to cherish them

**1:58 pm**

I think when you live past the point where you thought you were going to die , everything either feels like a bonus or burden

**4:44 sept 23**
You're sat in the rain
Sipping Fat Tires, lips pressed against the bottle
Ordered a burger and fries but waited to eat it
An act of discipline
A dance of satisfaction
Looks of contemplation
I wonder what you're thinking

**Sept 23rd, the end of summer 23**

To quench the thirst I have for you I'd drink dry the waters world wide, leaving not a drop,
then replenish them with tears when you relinquish your hold on me
because my gesture was just too much.

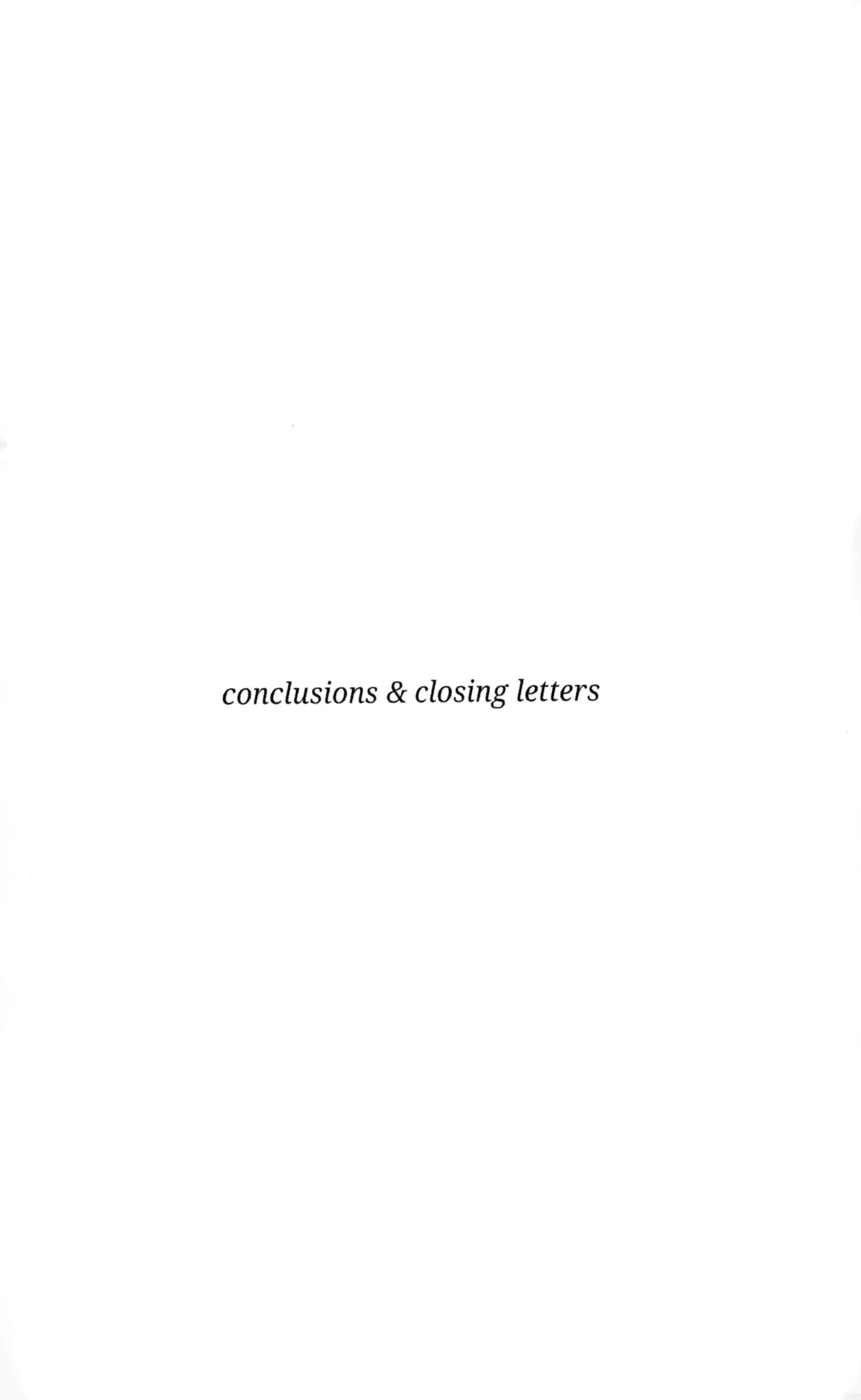

*conclusions & closing letters*

i.

***I promise you it will always be different.***

*I promise you, what is will be different than that which was before it.*

*Be honest. Be sincere. Tell the truth about what you felt then, what you feel now, and what you hope to feel moving forward. Energy is never created nor destroyed, just transferred and transformed. The energy of the past becomes a memory and that's that; all that energy can be is a memory. You've learned the alchemy of not letting that energy taint the present moment - hold that momentum going forward and teach that lesson in the love you share and the mindful kindness that you show when you accept this moment for what it is and make it known that the past does not effect the present. I promise you, what is will be different than that which was before it. That love, relationship, job, person, place, position, dream, thought- has changed since I had it, and since I've known you. These memories and foregone moments make us who we are, but are not who we are entirely. We are stories constantly being written. We are unfinished. Worry not about the chapters we've written, but let us put our minds together and see what wonderful world we can create going forward, together.*

ii.

you'll be settling in on that long ride. you'll stay seated for the people who didn't make it this far in the journey. they're counting on you; they live through you now. and it's not to put pressure on you, but to remind you, it's not just you in this. no matter how alone you feel, it is not just you. i want you to remember that. i want you to be proud of yourself for what you've done. for writing this, putting it together. i want this to be a reminder that when you relax, take a deep breath, sober up a bit and focus, there's nothing you can't do. i want your next 365 to be a textbook example of what it means to become dedicated. show what a 180 in direction looks like when you make a 180 in perspective. you have to look where you're heading, and look at where your head is. remember that you sleep where your bed is so be careful who you let in it. i'm proud of the work you're doing on yourself. keep doing it. i'm proud of the work you're about to do on yourself. keep doing it. and when we cross this finish line and start the next race and the entire world is watching us run with the wind at our backs, i'll be proud of the work you've done to get us there, just to be running and racing again. i love you, i'm proud of you, keep running, son.

iii.

to the person who's thinking of giving up, whatever that may look like, please don't. the world needs who ever it is that you're meant to be, what you're meant to write, create, say, film; the child you're going to raise, the doctor you would be. the world needs your smile at the checkout counter, the bar, office, the drive thru, the truck stop, the factory floor. we need you. we need your idea, so create it, share it, show it, write it. if you're 13, 23, 33, 63, 83, just do it, keep going. i'm going on 30 and so many times i've wanted to quit. i've wanted to give up. to roll over and let the life leave me, and i've tried, but it doesn't work. someone needs me, and i know that. i've got so much love in my heart for you and i believe in what you're trying to do. i'm specifically thinking of kids with a dream; kids who start at 14 and grind until they're 24 and don't see an end road in sight, that are 27 thinking of quitting because you're afraid of barely being started at 30. i just want to say that if you love what you're doing, whatever it is that you're doing, then what does any of that matter? dedicate yourself to your craft and loving others and to getting 1% better each day, and you'll be fine. doctors don't usually really get going until their 30s, why's it different for artists? Lean into it, embrace it, be who you are meant to be. be weird, have fun, be intentional. i'll be right there beside you doing the exact same thing.

i heard once that writing is not what you do, it's who you are. let yourself be who you are. be free to see more, feel more, observe more, love more, and know more. it makes for better, more honest writing. allow yourself to convey your world to others. let yourself fully feel the world around you.
i promise you, it's worth it in the end. *it's as deep as it is to you, and that's okay.*

*it may not feel like it,*
*but we were meant to feel this much*
*otherwise we'd be reading the poems*
*not writing them;*
*or not feeling the poems*
*when we read them.*

there is an angel who exists beside me, who sees the pain behind my writing, and loves me regardless. Thank GOD for sisters. I wouldn't be here without mine.
I Love You Gabrielle, thank you.

i know that it's been hard, but it will all get better.
i promise you, i'll see that it's true for you.

*a letter to my mother*

All the love I could have had that's passed like water through my glass, that's ran like sand out of my grasp, that's gone like thoughts I should have had and now-
Where are they now? These lost lovers of the shadows that are my early twenties, where are they now? Friends I can call and talk to or people who speak to me? Do you think of me, infrequently, on solemn Saturday mornings; are there memories of evenings drinking, watching as the sun is sinking with your body near me as we talk about what we've been thinking and sometimes dreaming? Do you think of me when you're sleeping and your mind is left to it's worst devices? Am I even a figment in my own imagination, nevertheless, a fading fabric in the quilt of the mind of someone else who *has* found happiness?

Am I the one who got away or just the one you stay away from? Do I even matter to you as much you ever mattered to me? maybe just an ounce of that reciprocated and I'd be living happily, too, but no, I'm alone in this room beside the water listening to the rapids, thoughts growing vapid, ever aware of your absence and I'm wondering:
Does anything matter at all, ever, or is it all random and people will choose who they choose for seemingly no purpose and when I'm finally laid to rest, have ascended the golden steps, God will greet me, arm around me, hand on my chest and say "it was funny, wasn't it? That you hypothesized a theory at 6 years old in Walmart and I showed you what it was like to be right your entire life?" And I'll sit in my

room full of many mansions and wonder if it was all really worth it. Oh how perfect, to be right, unless you're right that no one ever finds the proper person, that all promises are hallow, all rings are shallow and all marriages are gallows because no one's vows are hallowed. I'm astounded at this mountain of insurmountable evidence that we're always on the precipice, but only on the precipice,
of finding who we are meant to be and who we are meant to be with.

My hypothesis at 6 years old was in the form a question to my father when I saw two couples holding hands: "What if they're not supposed to be holding hands with the person they're with? What if they'd be happier if they were with someone else?
If we end up with the wrong person what happens?"

There is a life I've always wanted and always dreamed of having. Always, constantly, somewhere in my mind these desires are playing like a TV left on and forgotten about. A projector showing images to chairs in an empty room, cobwebs growing in the corners, across the projector lens, augmenting the film perspective but still rolling nevertheless. How this life taunts me daily through computer and phone screens, fed to me in movies and shows, teasing me through city streets as I travel or go back home. How many moments have I missed of that life, staggered and pushed back by the struggles of this one. Depression, complacency, fear strangle me- not to my death, just to the place of defending my breath. I have been struggling to breathe for years. Exasperated, I fear I'm coughing my final call to be rescued and delivered to the life I deserve. The call is to myself, to finally put in the work. The call is to God to remove the barriers, or show me how to hurdle. The call is to the universe to finally align. Years I've been grieving, eking out the flashes of my creativity when I can pull myself from the ashes of despair and depression. I lost everything and sometimes lay within the rubble. I know a phoenix rises from the ashes, but maybe I'm not meant to fly. That's not true though, I see the life meant for me. This is me reaching my hand out, one foot in the water, one sinking, two steps off the boat. See me, Lord, hand outstretched, and pull me forth. I know the prophecy and the purpose, I just don't get the journey or know what the point is. Maybe these poems make sense of it all when we look back on them. Maybe it's all for the greater good of everyone else, but I wish it would feel good to me for a season.

So instead of letting this life play on the projector in the empty room, I've brought my own projections and I'm showing them to you. These are letters to anyone who needs them. Anyone who reads them. These are letters to lost lovers, missed connections, passing moments that I loved dearly- my last letters to them (for the moment) as I hope to write new letters to people, moments and memories. I am one of my lost lovers, because I no longer love the version of me that I was. I want to write new letters to my new self. These are the last of these painful, joyful, twisted moments. A new season is upon us, so fill the seats, roll the film, and share with someone that you love these letters that I loathe.

But I love you, for reading them, and I'm grateful it's my book you chose.

Until I'm sad, happy, empty, or whole again,
Take Care,

-Ty